LEARN ABOUT VALUES

RESPONSIBILITY

by Cynthia Roberts

The
Child's
World®

Published in the United States of America by The Child's World®
1980 Lookout Drive • Mankato, MN 56003-1705 • 800-599-READ • www.childsworld.com

The Child's World®: Mary Berendes, Publishing Director; Katherine Stevenson, Editor
The Design Lab: Kathy Petelinsek, Art Director; Julia Goozen, Design and Page Production

Photo Credits: © Ariel Skelley/Corbis: 5; © iStockphoto.com/Jyn Meyer: 21; © Tim Pannell/Corbis: cover;
All other photos © David M. Budd Photography

Library of Congress Cataloging-in-Publication Data
Roberts, Cynthia, 1960–
  Responsibility / by Cynthia Roberts.
    p. cm. — (Learn about values)
  ISBN 978-1-59296-676-9 ISBN 1-59296-676-4 (library bound: alk. paper)
  1. Responsibility—Juvenile literature. 2. Values—Juvenile literature. I. Title. II. Series.
  BJ1451.R58 2006
  179'.9—dc22   2006000976

CONTENTS

What Is Responsibility?

Do you have jobs to do? Maybe you have to feed your dog every day. Maybe you have to make your bed. Responsibility is a duty or a job. Are you responsible for something? That means no one else will do it for you. You must take care of it yourself.

Pets are fun. They are also a big responsibility!

Responsibility at School

There are lots of jobs and rules at school. You need to do your homework on time. You need to keep your desk clean. You might have to feed the class goldfish. You show responsibility by doing these things without being told.

Being responsible means doing a good job.

Responsibility **at Home**

Maybe you have jobs to do at home. You must put your clothes away in the closet. You must take the garbage out after dinner. You must put your toys away before bedtime. Sometimes you do not like to do these things. But your family trusts you to be responsible. You do your jobs even when you do not want to.

Being responsible means taking care of the things around you.

Taking Care of Yourself

Being responsible means taking good care of yourself. You brush your teeth every morning. You comb your hair and wash your face. You do not have to be told to do these things. You show responsibility by doing them on your own.

Caring for yourself is an important responsibility!

Responsibility and Your Parents

Your parents make lots of rules you must follow. Your must clean your room. You must be home for dinner every night. You must go to bed on time. Your parents have good reasons for making these rules. They want to keep you happy and safe. You show responsibility by following their rules.

Being responsible is good for the whole family.

13

Responsibility and Your Friends

You and your friends want to open a lemonade stand. Each person is in charge of bringing something. One person needs to bring the pitcher. One person needs to make the sign. Your job is to bring the cups. You show responsibility by remembering your part.

Responsibility means following through.

Responsibility and Others

You can show responsibility to strangers, too! You can use the playground **equipment** the right way. You can be careful around the other kids. What if someone gets hurt anyway? You can show responsibility by getting help for them.

Being responsible means watching out for other people.

Responsibility and Your Neighborhood

Lots of people share your neighborhood. It is a nice place to live. Everyone needs to do their part to keep it that way! You can show responsibility by keeping your neighborhood clean. You can pick up trash and throw it away. You can **recycle** cans and bottles.

Being responsible makes a difference in how we live.

19

Responsibility Makes You a Better Person

When you show responsibility, people know they can count on you. They know you will do your job. They know you will do things the right way. And you will feel good about the things you do. You will know you have done your best.

Doing your best feels great!

glossary

equipment
Equipment is a set of tools or machines used to do something.

recycle
When you recycle something, you use it a second time.

books

Carlson, Nancy. *It's Not My Fault*. Minneapolis, MN: Carolrhoda Books, 2003.

Leaney, Cindy, and Peter Wilks. *Taking Care of Mango: A Story about Responsibility*. Vero Beach, FL: Rourke, 2003.

Loewen, Nancy, Brandon Reibeling, and Omarr Wesley. *Do I Have To?: Kids Talk About Responsibility*. Minneapolis, MN: Picture Window Books, 2002.

web sites

Visit our Web page for links about character education and values:
http://www.childsworld.com/links

Note to parents, teachers, and librarians:
We routinely check our Web links to make sure they're safe, active sites—so encourage your readers to check them out!

index

about the author

Even as a child, Cynthia Roberts knew she wanted to be a writer. She is always working to involve kids in reading and writing, and she loves spending time in the children's section of the library or bookstore. Cynthia enjoys gardening, traveling, and having fun with friends and family.